Trade Up: Dating and Relationships Without Settling

Copyright © 2025 by Dominic Weeks and Shaun Phillips

Published by Progression

Washington, D.C., United States

For permissions, inquiries, or bulk orders:

seasond.pro@gmail.com

ISBN: 9798297260450

Cover Design & Interior Layout by Progression

Printed in the United States of America

Table Of Contents

Acknowledgements

First and foremost, we want to thank **God**—the source of all clarity, healing, and elevation. Without divine guidance, we wouldn't have had the insight, strength, or conviction to write this book or walk these journeys.

To every person we've ever loved, lost, learned from, or let go of—you helped shape the perspective behind these pages. Whether the experience ended in heartbreak, healing, or harmony, you contributed to our evolution. Thank you for the lessons.

To the people who showed up for us when we were at our lowest—who reminded us of our worth when we forgot it— your presence was the difference between breaking and becoming. You are loved more than words can express.

To **Dominic Weeks**, co-author and real-life brother in growth—thank you for your honesty, vulnerability, and vision. This project wouldn't have existed without the real conversations and reflections we shared. Your ability to articulate what so many people feel but can't say is a rare gift. You brought wisdom, warmth, and truth to every chapter.

To our families—you are our roots. Every struggle, every breakthrough, every moment of doubt helped refine the men we've become. We carry your strength with us always.

To our readers—thank you for trusting us with your time, your attention, and most importantly, your heart. Whether you've dog-eared a single chapter or read this cover to cover, we hope these words helped you see your value more clearly and gave you permission to expect more—*from others, and from yourself.*

Lastly, to anyone out there who's ever felt like they had to settle in love, in friendship, or in life:
This book was for you.
And we hope it gave you the courage to trade up—for real.

With gratitude and respect,
Shaun Phillips & Dominic Weeks

Introduction

The Power of Connection

There's a reason we feel empty when we're disconnected.
Humans are wired for relationships—not just romance, but real, soul-stirring connection. The kind that affirms our worth, sharpens our thinking, brings us peace, and reminds us we're not alone on this journey.

But here's the problem:
Most people settle.
They stay in relationships that drain their energy, suppress their growth, and distort their vision of love, friendship, and even self-worth. Others isolate themselves completely, convincing themselves they're better off solo—while silently suffering in loneliness.

I've lived both of these truths.
I've been the person stuck in unbalanced relationships and the one avoiding them altogether. I've felt the weight of unmet expectations, awkward silences, emotional letdowns, and deep regret. But I've also experienced the opposite: high-value, soul-nourishing, mutually empowering relationships that changed my life.

And that's what this book is about.

Why Relationships Shape Everything

The quality of your relationships influences every other area of your life.

- Your mental health is shaped by the people you trust.
- Your emotional safety is shaped by the people you love.
- Your career trajectory is shaped by the people you surround yourself with.
- Even your self-worth is shaped—directly or indirectly—by your connections.

We can't afford to take relationships lightly. Whether romantic, professional, or platonic, each relationship in your life either brings you closer to your higher self—or distracts you from it.

Every relationship leaves a mark.
The question is: are you proud of those marks—or healing from them?

What It Means to "Trade Up"

To "Trade Up" means evolving.
It means stepping away from relationships rooted in guilt, trauma, or survival mode—and stepping into connections built on alignment, value, and reciprocity.

It's not about arrogance. It's not about playing games.
It's about choosing with clarity.
It's about being intentional with who gets access to your life, your energy, and your heart.

You're not just looking for someone to fill a space.
You're looking for someone who matches your growth, mirrors your effort, and contributes to your peace. And that requires self-awareness, reflection, and unshakable standards.

What You'll Get From This Book

This book is both a mirror and roadmap. It will challenge the beliefs that keep you stuck and provide tools to build something better. You'll learn how to:

- Identify and release low-value relationships
- Heal from trauma bonds and emotional baggage
- Audit your current circle with honesty and intention
- Attract emotionally mature, high-value connections
- Protect your peace and enforce powerful boundaries
- Sustain relationships that match the person you're becoming

Your Invitation to Level Up

You don't need permission to choose better.
You don't have to stay where love is withheld or conditional. You're allowed to change your circle. You're allowed to be selective. And you're allowed to believe that something healthier, deeper, and more aligned is possible for you.

This isn't about perfection. It's about progression.
If you're ready to upgrade not just who's in your life—but how you love, communicate, and connect—this book is for you.

Let's Trade UP. Let's do it with honesty, courage, and intentionality. Let's begin.

Chapter 1: You're Never Not in a Relationship

Every Relationship Leaves a Mark

There's no reason you should be depressed—and alone.
If you're sitting at home scrolling through your phone, envious of your friend with a new girlfriend or your best friend who's happily married with kids, that's not just normal—it's a wake-up call.

I've been there—lonely, misunderstood, bitter.
Dating felt like a Rubik's cube I couldn't solve. Social anxiety made it hard to speak up, let alone express my feelings. I knew what I wanted, but I didn't know how to create it. And worst of all, I felt like I was the only one going through it.

But here's the truth: every relationship you've ever had—romantic, platonic, professional—has shaped you.
Some have healed you. Others have hurt you. But they all taught you something.

The key is not to ignore those lessons, but to **reflect, evolve, and use them to build better connections going forward**.

Why Connection Matters More Than You Think

I have a friend who just turned 30. He's a good man with a strong heart, but he's completely opted out of dating. He's decided it's not worth it. I used to feel the same way. In my younger years, I was awkward around women, trapped by fear and uncertainty. I didn't know how to express what I wanted or how to connect in a way that felt authentic. It was frustrating and, at times, deeply discouraging.

But what I wish my friend—and every person hiding from connection—understood is this:

Our lives are built through relationships.
Every victory, every wound, every breakthrough we experience is connected to another person.

Even the *lack* of connection can be devastating.
According to CNN's segment, *"Why the Rate of Single Men Looking for Dates Has Declined,"* there's a growing crisis of loneliness among men that leads to everything from depression and self-doubt to suicidal ideation. And while this book isn't just for men, the implications are real for everyone.

You weren't meant to do life alone.
Not because marriage is the goal—but because **companionship is part of being human**.

The Three Core Relationship Types

To create balanced relationships, you first need to understand the roles people play in your life. Every relationship you have falls into one (or more) of three categories:

1. **Personal** – Family, friends, social connections
2. **Professional** – Coworkers, mentors, community networks
3. **Romantic** – Sexual, emotional, short-term or long-term

A healthy life is one where these relationships are aligned. You might be thriving professionally and personally but feel unfulfilled romantically. That imbalance creates emotional friction. One of my best friends is a respected medical professional with a booming social life—but she didn't make time for companionship. She became "the dog lady," and while she embraces it humorously, there was real loneliness behind that label.

Eventually, she and I had a heart-to-heart. She admitted that her career success didn't make up for the emptiness of not having someone to share her life with. Since then, she's started dating seriously—and she's happier. She's not seeking perfection—she's seeking **balance**.

Cutting Off What Doesn't Serve You

Equally important as finding the right relationships is letting go of the wrong ones.

We've all had people in our lives who drained us—emotionally, physically, financially. People who took and never gave. Who manipulated your kindness, overstayed their welcome, or blurred the lines between affection and entitlement.

You know who they are. You've probably given them chance after chance.

Rip. The. Band-Aid. Off.

Let me give you a real story.

I once went to Orlando, Florida, hoping to enjoy myself and maybe connect with a woman I'd been speaking to online. I paid for a nice hotel, a rental car, and took her out to multiple meals. But during our time together, she never offered to contribute financially, never showed interest in intimacy, and seemed content to just enjoy the ride on my dime. Eventually, I stood up for myself. I let her know I felt used and that I should've communicated my expectations more clearly. She respected that and left.

It wasn't about the money. It was about the **principle**.
I realized that if someone isn't bringing value—emotionally, spiritually, or practically—they don't belong in my inner circle.

Another time, a friend of mine came over. I found her attractive, and I was honest about wanting to be intimate. She told me that wouldn't happen unless we were in a relationship. I respected her honesty, and while I liked her personality, I didn't see a long-term future. So I didn't push it—and I didn't keep her around just to "see what happens." Years later, she got married—and I'm proud of her and proud of myself for respecting both of our boundaries.

Your Relationships Are Your Brand

Here's the part people forget:

Your relationships reflect your identity. They are an extension of your brand.

When I met my wife, I was struck by her ambition. She had a vision board, monthly goals, and a real strategy for her life. She wasn't just coasting—she was creating. Most of the women I had dated before her were in "survival mode." They had no plan, no clarity, and were just waiting for a "good man" to make life better.

I wanted more—and she was more.
She became part of my vision because she *already* had one.

Who you partner with—romantically, socially, professionally—either multiplies your potential or reduces it. If you choose someone who's emotionally unstable, irresponsible, or visionless, it reflects back on you.

So ask yourself:

- Does this person represent the future I want?
- Are they aligned with the brand I'm building?

If the answer is no, it's time to reassign their access to your life.

Conclusion: Relationships Aren't Optional—They're Foundational

You are never not in a relationship.
Even when you're alone, you're in relationship with yourself—and that sets the tone for everything else.

So make it count.

Choose people who add to your life, not subtract from it. Make space for companionship. Let go of what drains you. And most importantly, align your relationships with the best version of yourself.

Because if you're serious about leveling up your life—you'll need people beside you who are serious about *you*.

Chapter 2: What Is a High-Value Relationship?

Emotional, Mental, Spiritual, and Practical Value

Let's be real—no relationship is perfect.

I'm married, and even though my wife and I have a strong bond, we've had our share of tough moments. We've disagreed. We've argued. We've hit blind spots—whether from work stress, parenting challenges, or financial strain. I'm stubborn. She's passionate. Sometimes we clash. But despite all that, I love her deeply, and I respect her even more than I did when we first met.

Why?

Because we're in a **high-value relationship**.

A high-value relationship isn't about appearances or Instagram captions. It's about **how the relationship makes you feel, grow, and show up in the world**. It's about emotional safety, spiritual alignment, practical support, and a shared commitment to evolve.

Here's what defines a high-value relationship—and why you should never settle for less.

1. Emotional Intelligence Is the Glue

At the core of every strong relationship is emotional intelligence—also known as **EQ**.
EQ is the ability to:

- Understand and manage your own emotions
- Recognize and respond to the emotions of others
- Navigate conflict with empathy, not ego

When my wife is stressed, I can feel it before she says a word. Instead of ignoring her or telling her to "get over it," I try to step in—take our daughter out for a while, plan a date night, or just listen without trying to fix everything. And when I'm in a funk, I communicate it: "I need time to recharge." She respects my needs and gives me space to reset.

This mutual understanding is powerful.
We don't sweep things under the rug. We address them head-on—with care and respect. That's EQ in action.

2. Healthy Relationships Allow for Space and Balance

One of the best things about my marriage is that we give each other breathing room.
My wife goes out with her friends, invests in her hobbies, and regularly sees a therapist. I do the same. We have lives outside each other, and we support that freedom.

This isn't about separation—it's about balance.
It's about being able to refocus, recharge, and return to the relationship as your best self.

We've even done couples therapy. That's not a sign of weakness—it's a strategy for growth. Therapy gave us a neutral space to process emotions and create better communication habits.

In a high-value relationship, personal growth is welcomed—not feared.

3. Peace Is the Priority

Let me be clear:
My home is not a war zone. It's a sanctuary.

Yes, we argue. Yes, we disagree. But we **protect the peace**. We avoid toxic patterns like shouting, name-calling, or passive-aggressiveness. If one of us needs to walk away and cool down, we respect that.

In a world full of chaos, your home should be a place of peace.
If you're constantly bracing for emotional explosions, that's not love—it's survival mode. And it will drain you.

A high-value relationship is built on consistent calm, not occasional kindness.

4. Real Growth—As a Couple and as Individuals

The best relationships help both people grow.
That growth may be emotional, financial, spiritual, or even physical. You should look back over time and see:

- Better communication
- Healthier habits
- Shared progress toward goals

Even small improvements matter. Baby steps count. If you're with someone and your life is **stuck**—that's a sign the connection isn't nourishing your potential.

A high-value relationship isn't just about **feeling good**—it's about **getting better**, together.

Transactional vs. Transformational Bonds

Let's talk about two kinds of relationships that are easy to confuse:

✗ Transactional Bonds

These are based on one person's gain.
They might look good on the outside—fun dates, cute pictures, good sex—but at the core, they're empty. One person is giving way more than they're receiving. There's no depth, no real partnership.

I once dated a woman who seemed promising. I drove over an hour just to see her. I paid for everything. But when I had surgery and was on bed rest, she didn't visit, check in, or even send a meal. I realized—*this wasn't a partnership. I was just a convenience.*

I cut her off. And it was one of the best decisions I ever made.

■ Transformational Bonds

These are built on mutual respect, shared growth, and genuine care.

In my late 20s, I dated women who *gave back*. They checked on me. They celebrated my wins. They planned dates. They remembered the small things. That's what reciprocity looks like.

These relationships didn't just feel good—they helped me become a better man. And that's what made them transformational.

If a relationship doesn't help you level up emotionally, mentally, spiritually, or practically—it's not high-value. It's just familiar.

Your Relationship Standard Is a Mirror

Your standards in relationships reflect your **self-worth**.

I knew I was leveling up when I stopped tolerating inconsistency. I stopped justifying bad behavior. I stopped chasing people who didn't match my energy.

That's when the right people showed up.

You don't attract what you want. You attract what you're ready for.

Conclusion: Don't Just Want More—Require It

High-value relationships aren't rare. They're just rarely demanded.

If you want a love that feels like peace and progress—not confusion and chaos—you have to set a new standard. You have to value yourself enough to stop accepting surface-level connection.

- Require emotional intelligence.
- Require growth.
- Require peace.
- Require reciprocity.

Because once you've experienced a high-value relationship—there's no going back.

Chapter 3: The Psychology of Attachment and Connection

Why We Love the Way We Do

Let's keep it real.
The way you connect with people—especially in close relationships—isn't random. It's deeply influenced by how you were raised, how you were treated in your earliest relationships, and how you learned to survive emotionally.

Whether you're clingy, distant, guarded, or secure... it's not a flaw. It's a pattern. And that pattern has a name:

Attachment Style.

Attachment theory is one of the most important keys to understanding your relationship choices. Once you recognize your attachment style, you unlock a whole new level of self-awareness and relational clarity.

The Four Main Attachment Styles

1. Secure Attachment

The "Solid" Connection

You're able to trust, communicate, and connect without losing yourself. You can express needs, hear others out, and set boundaries without guilt.

- You're comfortable being close and also having space.
- You seek healthy relationships and respond well to challenges.
- You believe in your worth—and theirs.

How it affects your choices:

You tend to make balanced, thoughtful decisions. You're not scared to love deeply or walk away when necessary. Your relationships reflect your self-trust.

2. Anxious-Preoccupied Attachment

The "Nervous" Connection

You crave closeness—but you fear abandonment. You overthink. You constantly need reassurance. You may feel like you're "too much" or always on edge emotionally.

- You might become clingy or over-accommodating.
- You read too much into silence or small changes in behavior.
- You sometimes lose your identity in the pursuit of love.

How it affects your choices:

You may settle for less just to avoid being alone. You say "yes" when you want to say "no." You move too fast or stay too long in relationships that drain you.

3. Dismissive-Avoidant Attachment

The "Independent" Connection

You value freedom over intimacy. You avoid emotional depth. You downplay your needs and ignore those of others.

- You don't like depending on people.
- You keep relationships casual or surface-level.
- You shut down or ghost when things get intense.

How it affects your choices:
You choose logic over emotion. You fear vulnerability. You may leave before things get "too real"—even if the connection is good.

4. Fearful-Avoidant Attachment

📍 *The "Confused" Connection*
You want love—but you don't trust it. You crave closeness but fear being hurt. Your past experiences may have taught you to expect pain.

- ## You run hot and cold.
- ## You sabotage healthy connections.
- ## You feel unworthy of real love but terrified of being alone.

How it affects your choices:
Your decisions are inconsistent. You might pull someone in, then push them away. You confuse passion with chaos and fear stability will lead to boredom or betrayal.

My Story: From Anxious to Avoidant to Secure

As a teen, I was deep in anxious territory.
I grew up in a very conservative church. I followed the rules: no sex before marriage, no drinking, no gambling. Women were seen as delicate, pure, and put on a pedestal. That belief shaped how I approached relationships—I idolized women, feared rejection, and constantly craved their approval.

I didn't just want connection—I *needed* it to feel worthy.

But after years of rejection, social anxiety, and spiritual guilt, I flipped. I turned into a "playboy." I avoided commitment. I avoided emotional depth. I dated for fun, not for substance.

Then, in my late 20s, I met someone different. She was kind, grounded, and transformational. We had a beautiful relationship—but I still wasn't ready. I felt smothered by the intimacy. I left... not because she wasn't amazing, but because *I was dismissive-avoidant.*

It wasn't until my early 30s—after working on myself—that I finally felt ready. That's when I met my wife.

Secure attachment didn't come from someone else fixing me.
It came from me doing the inner work to **trust, open up, and stay grounded.**

Trauma Bonds vs. Healthy Attachments

Let's break down two very different—but often confused—types of emotional connection:

✗ Trauma Bond

A cycle of pain disguised as passion

A trauma bond happens when you're stuck in a rollercoaster relationship—high highs, low lows, constant confusion. These bonds often form with people who hurt you, manipulate you, or create chaos... but still occasionally throw you just enough love to keep you hanging on.

Signs of a trauma bond:

- Emotional whiplash: love-bombing one moment, cruelty the next
- You feel addicted to them—even when they mistreat you
- You feel isolated from friends, family, and reality
- You make excuses for their behavior
- You confuse intensity for intimacy

It's not love. It's survival. And it's exhausting.

■ Healthy Attachment

A safe, secure, mutual connection

A healthy attachment is built on **trust, communication, and emotional balance**. It creates a sense of peace, even when life is hard. It doesn't require performance. It allows for honesty. It strengthens your self-worth.

Signs of a healthy attachment:

- Mutual respect and space to grow
- Safe conversations, even about hard topics
- Shared emotional labor
- Consistency and dependability
- Encouragement to pursue your own goals

The difference? A trauma bond drains you. A healthy attachment fuels you.

Rewiring the Way You Relate

The good news?
Attachment styles are not fixed. You can rewire them.

Here's how:

1. **Identify Your Pattern**
   Are you anxious? Avoidant? Fearful? Secure? Awareness is step one.
2. **Trace It Back**
   What early experiences shaped your connection habits? Explore your upbringing, family dynamics, past relationships, and trauma.
3. **Challenge the Narrative**
   You are not unlovable. You are not too much. You are not unsafe in every relationship. Interrupt those beliefs.
4. **Build Self-Worth Internally**
   Journal. Meditate. Hit the gym. Go to therapy. Speak affirmations. Do the work that makes you feel whole *before*seeking connection.
5. **Practice Healthier Habits**
   Set boundaries. Ask for what you need. Be honest. Stay when it's safe. Walk away when it's not. Learn new love languages.
6. **Choose Secure People**
   Surround yourself with emotionally mature people. Their presence can literally retrain your nervous system to feel calm and safe.
7. **Seek Therapy if Needed**
   A trained therapist can help you unpack the deeper layers and rebuild your relationship blueprint.

Conclusion: You Can Heal How You Love

You are not broken.
You just learned how to protect yourself the best way you could. And now, you get to **unlearn what no longer serves you**.

Attachment styles don't define your destiny—they describe your starting point. With reflection, practice, and intention, you can rewrite your relational story.

Secure love isn't a fantasy. It's a frequency. And you can get there.

Chapter 4: Trade Up, Don't Settle

Stop Accepting What's Comfortable and Choose What's Aligned

It's time to say the hard truth out loud:

Too many people are stuck in low-value relationships because they're afraid of better.

They're not blind. They're not stupid. They're just scared—of change, of growth, of the unknown.

But here's what you need to know:
Settling for a partner who drains you is more dangerous than being alone. Choosing someone just because they're "familiar" is not loyalty—it's self-abandonment.

If you want a relationship that evolves, elevates, and energizes you... you're going to have to trade up. And that means outgrowing patterns, people, and even parts of yourself.

Why People Stay in Low-Value Relationships

Let's break this down. Most people don't settle because they want to. They settle because they're caught in one of these four traps:

1. They're Scared of Better

I've met women who've never experienced what emotional intelligence looks like in a relationship. They've never been taken to a 5-star restaurant, never been deeply listened to, and never had their dreams supported.

They *want* a high-value relationship—but they don't believe it's real.
So, they cling to what's familiar—even if it's beneath them.

Often, these individuals lack the social, emotional, or even spiritual tools to recognize, attract, or maintain something better. They don't need judgment. They need *awakening*.

2. They're Scared to Leave What They Have

I once had feelings for a woman who was dating a man I could only describe as... a loser. No ambition. No growth. Just drifting through life. I expressed my interest, hoping she'd leave him.

She didn't.
She stayed with him for a while longer before eventually moving on—but not to me. And even now, she's still dating low-value men.

Why? Because she was comfortable. She feared disruption. She feared the risk that something better might not work out.

It's a common trap: **we romanticize the potential of people we're familiar with while ignoring the opportunity of people who would actually grow with us.**

3. They're Scared to "Glow Up"

Let's be honest—trading up requires *you* to level up too.

My wife is a movement all on her own.
She had assets before we met. She was a business owner. She traveled, networked, and built a life she was proud of. She didn't *need* me—she *chose* me.

That was intimidating at first. But instead of shrinking, I chose to grow.

Being with her made me a better man—more confident, more focused, more disciplined, and more financially aware. But I had to rise to that level.

Sometimes we settle because we're afraid of who we'd have to become to be worthy of better.

4. They Don't Know Their Worth

This is the biggest block of all.
If you don't believe you deserve healthy love, respect, support, or emotional safety—you'll never demand it. You'll normalize disrespect. You'll excuse inconsistency. You'll stay small.

I used to think I wasn't attractive enough. I felt "ugly" instead of "worthy." I accepted bad behavior because deep down, I didn't think I could do better.

But something shifted.

I started dressing better. I hit the gym. I started doing things that made me proud to be myself. And I started attracting people who reflected the version of me I was becoming—not the version I used to be.

Recognizing and Rebuilding Your Worth

Let's get practical.

Here are 6 actionable ways to start reclaiming your value:

1. Define Your Own Worth

You are not a reflection of your relationship status. You're not just someone's partner—you are whole on your own. Start there.

2. Believe You Deserve More

Say it out loud: *"I deserve peace, passion, and respect."* And mean it. Internalize it. Because if you don't believe it, no one else will either.

3. Focus on What You Can Control

You can't fix the dating scene. You can't fix broken people. But you *can* fix your mindset, your choices, your environment, and your energy.

4. Accept Yourself Fully

Stop waiting to be perfect. Love yourself now. Because self-acceptance is what makes you magnetic—it's what separates the desperate from the desirable.

5. Challenge the Negative Voice

Silence the voice that says you're "too much" or "not enough." Replace it with affirmations that root you in your power.

6. Invest in Yourself

Work out. Read books. Travel. Go to therapy. Start the business. Clean up your diet. Leveling up doesn't just attract better people—it aligns you with a better version of yourself.

What Happens When You Stop Settling

When you stop settling, you'll be tested.

People from your past will come back. Old temptations will resurface. You'll have to say no to "almost right" to make room for *truly aligned*.

But you'll feel lighter. Clearer. More powerful. And yes—lonelier at times. But the peace that comes from living in alignment is worth more than the company that drains you.

Conclusion: You Don't Just Deserve More—You Can Have It

Settling feels safe—but it steals your future.

The moment you raise your standard, the world shifts around you.
You attract different conversations. Different energy. Different opportunities. Different love.

And it starts with a decision:

I will no longer tolerate relationships that don't honor who I am and where I'm going.

Say it with your boundaries. Say it with your choices. Say it with your glow.

It's time to Trade Up.

Chapter 5: Audit Your Circle

"Not everyone deserves front-row seats in your life." – Shaun Phillips

You are the average of the five people you spend the most time with.
This isn't just a catchy quote—it's a psychological principle backed by decades of research. The people in your life shape your **thoughts**, regulate your **emotions**, and influence your **identity**, **decisions**, and **direction**.

If you're serious about trading up in life, you must take inventory of your relationships with ruthless honesty. Because...

Your circle is either your anchor or your launchpad.

The Hidden Influence of Your Circle

Social psychologist Dr. David McClelland found that your reference group—the people you associate with—determines up to **95% of your success or failure in life.**

Let that sink in.
Not your degree. Not your job. Not your talent.
Your *circle.*

Real Example:

When entrepreneur Lisa moved from her small hometown to Atlanta, she noticed an immediate shift.
"Back home, every conversation was about drama, bills, and how hard life was. When I changed my environment, people talked about healing, business, and legacy. I leveled up fast. It felt like my mind could finally breathe."

You are not immune to the emotional energy of those around you.
Your nervous system *adapts* to the dominant frequency of your environment—whether it's inspiring or draining.

The Relationship Audit: Who's in Your Life and Why?

It's time to conduct a **relationship audit**.
Ask yourself:

- What role does this person play in my life?
- How do I feel after interacting with them?
- Are they helping me grow or holding me back?

To make this easier, use the following four categories:

◆ 1. Expanders

These people challenge you, uplift you, and stretch your thinking. They bring creativity, encouragement, vision, and accountability.

"Being around them makes me want to become the best version of myself."

◆ 2. Drainers

These relationships are rooted in guilt, manipulation, or obligation. You often leave them feeling anxious, heavy, or unseen.

"I feel like I can't say no to them—even when I want to."

3. Maintainers

These are neutral relationships. There's no major conflict, but no real growth either. They might be rooted in habit, history, or convenience.

"We've been friends for years, but we don't really push each other."

▼ 4. Saboteurs

These are the most dangerous. They disguise themselves as allies but consistently undermine your progress—through backhanded compliments, passive-aggressiveness, jealousy, or subtle sabotage.

"They smile to my face, but their energy shifts when I talk about my wins."

The Science of Emotional Contagion

Dr. Elaine Hatfield's research on **emotional contagion** proves that emotions are contagious—like a virus. If you're constantly around negativity, pessimism, or chaos, you'll absorb it subconsciously.

In fact, studies show that simply sitting next to a highly stressed person can raise your **cortisol levels**.

This is why your circle matters.
Your *nervous system* depends on it.

Don't Confuse History With Value

One of the most toxic lies we tell ourselves is:

"But I've known them forever."

History doesn't equal alignment.
Just because someone was right for your **past** doesn't mean they belong in your **future**.

Loyalty without alignment creates internal conflict.

Real Example:

Jared had been friends with his college roommate for over a decade. But every time he shared a success, his friend would make a joke, change the subject, or subtly downplay it.
"I realized I was holding on to a ghost," Jared said.
Letting go wasn't about hate. It was about healing.

How to Conduct Your Relationship Audit

Grab a sheet of paper and divide it into four columns:

Name	Role (Expander, Drainer, etc.)	How I Feel After Interaction	Keep, Limit, or Release?
Jasmine	Expander	Motivated, clear	Keep
Sean	Drainer	Anxious, frustrated	Limit
Andre	Saboteur	Defensive, insecure	Release

But What If It's Family?

Tough truth:
Family titles don't guarantee healthy dynamics.

If someone constantly crosses boundaries, triggers emotional wounds, or disrupts your peace—you are allowed to limit access.

You don't have to cut them off to cut them back.

Access is earned—not assumed.

Emotional ROI: Return on Investment

Start thinking of your energy like a bank account.

- Who gives you a return?
- Who's constantly making withdrawals?
- Who's overdrafted their access?

If your relationships aren't bringing you peace, clarity, or support—it's time to reassess the investment.

Reflection Questions

Ask yourself:

- Who drains me emotionally, but I keep around out of guilt?
- Which relationships consistently fuel my growth?
- Who have I outgrown, but still give full access to?
- What conversations am I avoiding that would set me free?
- Where in my life do I feel the need to shrink to keep the peace?

Conclusion: Trade Up, Not Just In

You are not being mean.
You are being intentional.

Choosing better relationships is not about arrogance. It's about alignment.

Every time you audit your circle, you get clearer about who belongs in your future—and who belongs in your past. And when you **trade up**, you don't lose love...

You gain **peace**.

Chapter 6: Letting Go with Power

"Sometimes the most powerful thing you can do is walk away—with love, with peace, and with no need to explain."

The Real Cost of Holding On

Letting go is hard.
Not because we don't know it's time, but because we're afraid of what comes next.

We hold on out of guilt. Out of loyalty. Out of fear of being alone.
But here's the truth:

Staying in misaligned relationships doesn't make you noble. It makes you stuck.

The cost of staying in what no longer serves you is far higher than the discomfort of release.
You can't build a new future while clinging to expired connections.

Why Letting Go Feels So Hard

1. Emotional Bonds Are Addictive

Neuroscience shows that love and attachment activate the brain's **reward system**—specifically the dopamine and oxytocin pathways.
That's why toxic or inconsistent relationships can feel like *addiction*—you're chemically bonded to the *potential*, not the reality.

A Rutgers study even found that **heartbreak activates the same brain regions as drug withdrawal.**

So if letting go feels like withdrawal—it is.

2. We Mistake Familiarity for Safety

Humans crave routine—even painful ones.
Psychologist Dr. Joe Dispenza explains that many people prefer the discomfort they know over the unknown they fear.
That's why people stay in dysfunction.
Not because it's good, but because it's *predictable*.

But **familiar doesn't mean aligned.**
You can outgrow someone and still love them. You can choose peace over proximity.

What Letting Go Actually Means

Letting go isn't always about cutting people off.
It's about reclaiming your energy, your power, and your peace.

It can look like:

- Releasing the need to "fix" someone
- Detaching your self-worth from their validation
- Letting go of the fantasy version of them
- Creating emotional or physical space
- Walking away without waiting for closure

Letting go is not about proving them wrong—it's about proving yourself worthy.

Real-Life Vignette: The Breakup That Wasn't Ugly

Tasha had been dating her boyfriend for three years.
On paper, they looked perfect. But behind closed doors, she felt dismissed and emotionally unsupported.

"I thought I needed a *big* reason to leave—like cheating or abuse," she said. "But eventually, I realized that being unhappy was reason enough."

She ended things without blame, without bitterness, and without drama.
"I didn't need him to be the villain. I just needed to choose me."

Letting go with power means you don't need chaos to validate your exit.
Peace is a reason too.

How to Know When It's Time to Let Go

Ask yourself:

- Do I feel emotionally smaller around this person?
- Does their presence shrink my growth?
- Am I walking on eggshells more than walking in love?
- Have I communicated my needs—and nothing's changed?
- Am I staying out of obligation, not alignment?

If the answer is yes, it's time to choose clarity.

"When someone shows you who they are, believe them the first time." – Maya Angelou

Letting Go of Guilt, Too

Many people stay because they feel guilty. Especially in family or long-term relationships.

But guilt is often a symptom of being raised to **prioritize other people's comfort over your own well-being**.

Reframe the guilt:

- ✗ "They'll be hurt if I walk away."
- ■ "They may feel hurt, but I'm allowed to protect my peace."

As therapist Dr. Nedra Glover Tawwab says:

"Guilt is often the price people pay for honoring their boundaries in dysfunctional systems."

Tools to Let Go with Power

1. Create a Closure Ritual

Closure doesn't always come from a final conversation. Sometimes, it comes from you.

Try:

- Writing a letter you'll never send
- Speaking your goodbye aloud in a quiet room
- Lighting a candle and releasing the emotional tie
- Archiving or deleting old photos, messages, or social media threads

Closure isn't a gift they give you—it's a decision *you* make.

2. Use the Circle of Access Strategy

Visualize your life as a set of concentric circles:

- **Inner Circle** – Full emotional access
- **Personal Circle** – Selective access
- **Social Circle** – Casual engagement
- **No Access** – Total boundary

Where does this person truly belong?
Maybe they were in the inner circle. Now, they need to be social—or even removed completely.

That's not punishment. It's *protection*.

3. Scripted Language for Graceful Letting Go

You don't need the perfect words. You just need clarity.

Here are a few you can borrow:

- "I'm choosing to take space to focus on my growth."
- "This connection no longer feels aligned, but I wish you well."
- "I don't have any anger—just clarity."

No explanation is owed. Just respectful truth.

What Comes After Letting Go

Grief. Doubt. Silence. Peace. Lightness. Loneliness.
It's all normal.

Letting go is both a funeral and a rebirth.
You're burying the version of you that tolerated misalignment—and stepping into the version of you that demands better.

The space you create becomes the soil for aligned relationships to grow.

Reflection Prompts

- What am I afraid will happen if I let this person go?
- What part of me still seeks their validation or approval?
- What would peace look like without this relationship?
- What do I gain—not lose—by releasing this bond?

Conclusion: Power Is Peace

Letting go with power isn't cold—it's conscious.
It means choosing clarity over confusion, peace over performance, and freedom over fear.

Yes, it might cost you some people.
But it will reward you with *yourself*.

You're not obligated to be emotionally available to people who've proven they can't handle your heart.
In the next chapter, we'll explore how to **choose who gets access** to your energy, emotions, and presence—because peace begins with **boundaries**.

Chapter 7: Choosing Who Gets Access

"Your peace is sacred. Not everyone deserves a key."

You Are the Gatekeeper

So many people spend their lives trying to be liked, included, and accepted...
That they forget: **you get to choose who has access to you.**

Your emotional availability is not a public park.

It's a gated sanctuary.

The more intentional you become about who gets to enter your emotional, mental, and physical space, the more peace and clarity you'll experience. You don't need 100 people cheering you on. You need *a few solid people* who truly see, respect, and support you.

Access Is a Privilege—Not a Right

Access isn't about love. You can love someone and still set limits.

What matters is **alignment**:

- How they show up in your life
- How they treat your energy
- How they respond to your growth

Just because someone has history with you doesn't mean they're entitled to intimacy. Time served is not a reason to stay.

Proximity ≠ Priority
Familiarity ≠ Fit

Scientific Insight: The Dunbar Number

Anthropologist **Robin Dunbar** found that humans can only maintain about:

150 social connections
50 close contacts
15 good friends
5 intimate relationships

That means not everyone *can* be close to you—and not everyone *should*.

Your energy is limited. Your time is valuable.
Be selective.

The Four Levels of Access

Imagine your life as a series of concentric circles. Each one represents a different level of emotional access:

🔒 1. Inner Circle (Core Access)

These are your most trusted people.
They know your fears and your dreams. They hold you accountable. They support your healing. They tell you the truth —with love.

Traits:

- Consistent
- Emotionally safe
- Trustworthy
- Growth-oriented

"These are the ones who know your battles and still believe in your brilliance."

⬤ 2. Personal Circle

These are solid friends, good colleagues, or spiritual family.
They matter—but they don't get full access to your inner life. There are boundaries.

"They see parts of your life, but not all of it."

⬤ 3. Social Circle

Neighbors, old classmates, online connections, friendly acquaintances.
You're cool—but not close. You're warm—but not vulnerable.

"We smile, but we don't share secrets."

⬤ 4. No Access

These are toxic, unsafe, or misaligned individuals.
They may have once been close—but their presence now causes chaos or tension.

"I can love you—and still love you from a distance."

How to Reassign Access

Ask yourself:

- How do I feel after interacting with this person?
- Do I trust them with my vulnerability?
- Do they encourage my growth or resent it?
- Do they respect my voice and boundaries?

If someone triggers anxiety, resentment, or guilt—*they don't belong in your Inner Circle.*

You are not being cold. You are being *clear.*

Real Example: The Quiet Repositioning

After Andre built a six-figure business, he noticed one of his oldest friends growing distant.
Any time Andre shared a win, his friend made slick comments like, "Must be nice," or "You changed."

Instead of arguing or cutting him off, Andre simply **repositioned** him.
They still talk—but not about goals, business, or anything personal.

"I stopped giving him front-row seats to my life. He didn't earn that view anymore."

Digital Access Is Emotional Access

Boundaries don't stop at your front door. They apply to your phone, your social media, and your inbox too.

If someone:

- Constantly texts you in crisis
- Follows you online but throws shade in real life
- Consistently drains you through DMs or comments

...it's okay to **mute, unfollow, or block.**

Your digital space is still your energetic space.

You don't owe digital access to anyone who disrespects your peace.

What to Do When You Outgrow Someone

You may not have beef. You may not be angry. You may just feel... misaligned.

And that's enough.

You can shift the relationship without drama:

- Reduce how often you reach out
- Stop oversharing
- Change the topics you discuss
- Reposition them in your mental and emotional landscape

Outgrowing someone doesn't mean you hate them.
It means your paths no longer walk side-by-side.

When They Notice the Distance

You might hear things like:

- "Why don't we talk like we used to?"
- "You acting brand new."
- "You switched up."

Here's how to respond with grace and clarity:

- "I'm just being more intentional with my time and energy."
- "I'm focused on alignment right now. No hard feelings."
- "Nothing's wrong. I'm just growing differently."

You don't owe explanations.
Only truth.

Your Access Is an Invitation to Your Peace

You don't need a big circle.
You need a solid one.

Choosing who gets access is about:

- Protecting your peace
- Honoring your boundaries
- Aligning your relationships with your future

The fewer people you give unfiltered access to, the clearer your life becomes.

Reflection Prompts

- Who currently has more access to me than they've earned?
- Who supports me without judgment or competition?
- Where am I shrinking to maintain a connection?
- What boundaries need to be enforced or reassessed?

Conclusion: You Get to Choose

You are not selfish for protecting your peace.
You are not arrogant for setting high standards.
You are not cruel for distancing yourself from confusion and chaos.

You are the gatekeeper of your emotional energy.
And when you *own that role*, you stop chasing validation—and start living in alignment.

In the next chapter, we'll explore how to **attract better relationships**—by becoming the kind of person your ideal connection is already searching for.

Chapter 8: How to Attract Better Relationships

"You don't chase what's meant for you. You become it—and it finds you."

Relationships Reflect Who You Are Becoming

Most people focus on **finding** better relationships.
But here's the truth:

The most powerful relationships are not found. They're *attracted*.

Healthy love, deep friendships, powerful partnerships—they aren't luck.
They're the natural result of living in alignment with your values, your worth, and your evolution.

If you want better, you must become better.
Not better than anyone else—better than the previous version of yourself.

You don't attract what you want.
You attract *what you are aligned with.*

The Law of Alignment

Relational neuroscience shows that we are wired to seek out relationships that mirror our internal beliefs.

- If you believe you're unworthy, you'll tolerate people who confirm that.
- If you believe you're valuable and growing, you'll attract people who rise to meet you.

Your energy is a filter. It calls in who's ready—and repels who's not.

If your relationships haven't upgraded, it's not always about others.
It's about where you are vibrating, healing, and standing.

Heal First, Then Call It In

We all say we want trust, consistency, and deep connection.
But many of us are still carrying emotional wounds that block what we claim to want.

Before you attract something better—you must become someone new.

Healing is not just self-care. It's preparation.

You cannot attract:

- honesty while tolerating liars
- peace while chasing chaos
- depth while settling for surface

Therapist Nedra Glover Tawwab writes,

"You teach people how to treat you by what you allow, what you stop, and what you reinforce."

Healing changes what you tolerate—and therefore, what you attract.

Real Example: Healing Became the Magnet

After a toxic breakup, Keisha spent a full year working on herself.
She went to therapy. She stopped people-pleasing. She reconnected with her passions.

"I wasn't even dating," she said. "I just focused on becoming the version of me that I loved."

Then, without forcing it, she met Elijah.
He was emotionally mature, secure, peaceful.

"He didn't complete me. He *met me* where I was already whole."

That's attraction at its highest level.
Not desperation. Not chasing.
Alignment.

How to Become Magnetic to Better Relationships

1. Embody What You Want

Whatever you desire—*become it first.*

- Want loyalty? → Be loyal to your values.
- Want peace? → Be peace in your own life.
- Want emotional safety? → Speak and hold truth, even when it's hard.

You can't demand from others what you deny in yourself.

2. Raise Your Standards—and Enforce Them

High standards are meaningless if you don't protect them.

- Don't flirt with red flags.
- Don't entertain "potential."
- Don't stay where inconsistency lives.

Standards without enforcement become suggestions.
And low-effort people will always test the limits.

3. Curate Your Energy

Your energy introduces you before your words do.

- Show up clear and centered.
- Stop dimming your light to make others comfortable.
- Stop over-explaining your growth.
- Get comfortable in your own company.

The more at peace you are in solitude, the less likely you'll entertain relationships that disturb it.

Scientific Insight: Attachment Repatterning

According to Dr. Sue Johnson, creator of Emotionally Focused Therapy, we can **repattern** our attachment styles over time.

With intentional healing and safe relationships, people who were once anxious or avoidant can become secure.

That means:

- If you've never experienced healthy love, you *can learn to give and receive it*
- If you've only known chaos, you *can learn peace*

As you grow, your relationships will begin to **mirror the version of you that's finally free.**

Affirmations That Shift Attraction

Speak these often:

- "I attract relationships that feel like peace, not pain."
- "I am worthy of consistency, clarity, and care."
- "My boundaries protect my energy and invite alignment."
- "I don't chase. I align—and I receive."
- "Every day, I become a magnet for healthy love."

Words shape belief. Belief shapes behavior. Behavior shapes attraction.

Reflection Prompts

- What kind of people have I been attracting—and what does that reveal about me?
- What patterns am I still healing before I invite someone new into my life?
- What standards do I need to reinforce more consistently?
- Who would I attract *if I fully loved, respected, and honored myself?*

Conclusion: Attraction Is Strategy, Not Luck

The love, peace, partnership, and intimacy you desire?
It's not out of reach.

But it's not something you chase. It's something you attract—through clarity, healing, alignment, and elevated energy.

The better you become, the better you attract.
And as you grow, you'll notice something powerful:

You no longer entertain what once drained you.
You no longer beg for what you once chased.
And the right relationships... just *flow.*

In the next chapter, we'll talk about **relationships that return**—and how to discern if it's a healthy reconnection or just a rerun of an old cycle.

Chapter 9: Relationships That Return Stronger

"Sometimes a goodbye is really a growth pause—meant to prepare you both for something better."

When They Come Back

Not all endings are permanent.
Friends fall off. Lovers separate. Family members become distant.
And sometimes, unexpectedly... they come back.

But here's the question you must ask:

Are they coming back evolved—or just familiar?

Time apart does not automatically equal growth.
Just because someone returns doesn't mean they're ready.

The Myth of "Bad Timing"

We love to romanticize reconnection.
"It just wasn't the right time."
"If only we met now instead of then."

While timing *can* be a factor, it's not the *main* one.

Growth, accountability, and emotional maturity are what make reconnection healthy—not just time.

A study published in the *Journal of Social and Personal Relationships* found that on-again/off-again relationships tend to have lower satisfaction and higher toxicity unless both people actively address what caused the original split.

If nothing changed, nothing changed.

Why Some People Return

Let's be honest—people don't always come back because they've evolved.
Here's what might really be happening:

- **They've done the work.** They've healed, reflected, and grown. They take ownership of their past behavior.
- **They miss your energy.** Not because they're ready—but because life is harder without you.
- **They see you glowing.** You've leveled up. Now they want access to the new you—without doing their own work.
- **They're lonely.** They're idealizing the past. They want comfort, not connection.

Only the **first reason** is worth entertaining.

Real Example: The Return That Worked

Trent and Simone dated in college. They were young, immature, and communication was poor. After breaking up, they went their separate ways—but both committed to personal growth.

Six years later, they reconnected at a mutual friend's wedding.

"We didn't pick up where we left off—we built something new," Simone said.
"We had both done therapy, healed, and evolved. It wasn't nostalgia. It was *alignment.*"

Now married with a child, they credit their success to **growing separately before reconnecting.**

Signs the Relationship Has Truly Evolved

- ■ They acknowledge past harm—no excuses or gaslighting
- ■ They show new behavior—not just new words
- ■ You feel safe in their presence—not triggered
- ■ The connection feels fresh—not like an old story replaying
- ■ Boundaries are respected—not resented
- ■ They're patient—not rushing back into old dynamics

"When the energy is healed, the connection feels different—even if it's the same person."

Red Flags in Reconnecting Relationships

- ▶ They act like nothing happened
- ▶ They use guilt, nostalgia, or "unfinished business" as bait
- ▶ They want instant access without rebuilding trust
- ▶ Their actions don't match their words
- ▶ You feel anxiety creeping back in

Old energy with new packaging is still old energy.

Checklist: Are They Ready or Just Returning?

Question	Healthy Answer
Have they acknowledged past harm?	"Yes, they took full ownership."
Have they shown consistent new behavior?	"Yes, it's visible—not just talk."
Do I feel emotionally safe and grounded around them?	"Yes, I don't have to shrink or perform."
Are we aligned in this new season of life?	"Yes, we're growing in the same direction."
Am I letting them back out of love—or loneliness?	"It's love—not fear."

Be honest. The future depends on it.

Reconnection vs. Repetition

A **reconnection** is based on healing, maturity, and clarity.
It feels peaceful. Slow. Honest.

A **repetition** is based on emotional addiction.
It feels intense. Fast. Confusing.

If the relationship feels like an old emotional loop—you're likely caught in repetition, not renewal.

"Sometimes God doesn't remove people to punish you. He removes them so they can grow beyond your reach—and only return when they're ready to meet you where you are now."

Rebuilding Takes Time

If someone's really changed, they'll be patient.

They won't:

- Demand full access immediately
- Rush your forgiveness
- Expect things to pick up where they left off

They'll prove themselves with presence—not promises.

Reflection Prompts

- Am I considering this reconnection out of growth or habit?
- What feels new about this connection—and what still feels familiar?
- What boundaries do I need to keep in place if we reconnect?
- If this doesn't work again, will I still be at peace with myself?

Conclusion: Sometimes They Come Back Different—And So Do You

Not every reconnection is a relapse.
Some are reunions with a **healed version of the bond**—a bond that couldn't thrive until both people grew separately.

The key is discernment.
Not everyone deserves a second chance—but some do. Just make sure that if they return...

They're not meeting the old you.
They're rising to the *new* you.

In the final chapter, we'll explore how to **sustain** high-value relationships—so you don't just trade up once...

You **stay up for life.**

Chapter 10:
Staying Up — Sustaining High-Value Relationships

"Attracting better relationships is one thing. Sustaining them is the real success."

Leveling Up Is Easy. Staying Up Takes Discipline.

Anyone can have a great first date.
Anyone can impress someone for a few months.
Anyone can post pictures and play the part of a healthy relationship.

But sustaining high-value connections—whether romantic, platonic, or professional—requires *intention*, *accountability*, and *emotional skill*.

You don't just want better relationships.
You want relationships that **last**.

This chapter is about how to keep what you've built.
Because once you've traded up, it's no longer about who they are.
It's about who you *continue becoming together*.

The Fallacy of Arrival

Many people treat great relationships like destinations:
"I found someone solid. I'm good now."

But connection is not a finish line.
It's a **living system**—one that must be nurtured, checked in on, and evolved.

Just like your body needs movement, your relationships need *maintenance*.

That means:

- Regular communication
- Emotional check-ins
- Conflict resolution
- Shared growth goals
- Personal accountability

Core Pillars of Sustainable Connection

Let's break down what truly holds a high-value relationship together.

1. Safety

Not physical safety—*emotional* safety.

"I can speak my truth without fear of punishment."
"I can bring my emotions without being dismissed."
"I can disagree without being attacked."

This is the foundation of **psychological trust**. Without it, people shut down, walk on eggshells, or become emotionally guarded.

2. Growth

High-value relationships are not just comforting—they're *challenging*.

They inspire self-reflection, call you higher, and hold you accountable.

You don't grow *in spite* of the relationship—you grow *through* it.

"We're not perfect, but we push each other toward better."
"We check each other with love and support."
"We evolve—together."

3. Boundaries + Freedom

Healthy relationships are not about ownership. They're about *honored autonomy*.

This means:

- Having personal space and passions
- Honoring individual healing journeys
- Supporting each other's independence
- Communicating when boundaries shift

Love is not surveillance. It's support.

4. Repair Over Ego

Conflict will happen. It's not a sign of failure—it's a sign of *aliveness*.

What matters is how you handle it.

- Can you apologize without defensiveness?
- Can you listen without needing to be "right"?
- Can you reconnect after disagreement without shame or withdrawal?

True emotional maturity is found in how quickly you *repair*, not how well you *avoid* tension.

"Healthy people don't avoid conflict. They *grow* through it."

Real Example: The Weekly Check-In

Angela and Marcus, a married couple, have a ritual every Sunday evening: a 15-minute emotional check-in.

They ask:

- "How are we doing?"
- "Did anything I said or did feel off this week?"
- "What do you need more of from me right now?"

It's simple. But it's powerful.

"We stopped letting resentment build," Angela said.
"We don't just love each other—we *manage* our relationship like it matters."

How to Maintain High Standards in Friendship Too

This isn't just for romantic partners.
Friendships need maintenance too.

Friend check-ins can look like:

- "Are we both showing up in this friendship?"
- "Do we still feel aligned?"
- "Is there anything we're not saying?"

Just like plants die from neglect, so do connections.
Water them—or be honest and let them go.

Signs You're Sustaining a High-Value Relationship

- You feel **safe** being fully yourself
- You're growing emotionally, mentally, and spiritually
- You can disagree with **respect**
- There's mutual effort—not just convenience
- You both *choose* each other repeatedly

It's not always perfect—but it's *real*.

Reflection Prompts

- Am I doing my part to maintain this connection?
- Are we still aligned in vision, values, and emotional energy?
- What does this relationship need more of right now?
- Where have I gotten too comfortable and stopped nurturing it?

Conclusion: Build to Last

Trading up isn't about showing off.
It's about **showing up**—consistently, consciously, and courageously.

The most meaningful relationships won't be built on drama, adrenaline, or fantasy.
They'll be built on *small daily choices*, emotional intelligence, and real alignment.

You've done the work to level up.
Now it's time to **stay up**—with people who match your healing, honor your boundaries, and grow beside you.

Because ultimately...

You don't just want connection. You want *legacy-level* **love.**
And that starts not just by attracting better—but by sustaining what's sacred.

Bonus Resources

Practical Tools to Apply What You've Learned

🔍 Self-Assessment: Relationship Alignment Audit

Use this quick quiz to assess the health and alignment of any relationship in your life—romantic, platonic, or professional.

For each question, rate from 1 (Never) to 5 (Always):

- I feel emotionally safe with this person.
- I can express myself without fear of judgment.
- Our relationship supports my growth and peace.
- This person respects my boundaries.
- I feel energized, not drained, after interactions.
- We resolve conflict in healthy, respectful ways.
- I'm not shrinking, walking on eggshells, or performing.
- Our connection is based on mutual effort—not obligation.

Scoring:

> 35–40: High-value, aligned relationship
>
> 25–34: Mixed alignment—needs honest reflection
>
> Below 25: Misaligned—consider reassessing access

🗨 Journal Prompts for Inner Work

These prompts help uncover patterns, build awareness, and strengthen your standards:

- What patterns have I repeated in relationships that no longer serve me?
- What do I believe I deserve in love and connection?
- What red flags have I ignored in the past—and why?
- Who in my life drains me, and who restores me?
- What boundaries do I struggle to hold—and with whom?
- What would a relationship built on alignment feel like for me?

💬 Powerful Boundaries Script Bank

Here are a few clear, respectful ways to enforce boundaries without guilt:

- "I value our connection, but I need more consistency if this is going to work."
- "I don't feel emotionally safe when you speak to me that way. I'm asking for respect."
- "I'm not available for one-sided friendships anymore."
- "I've changed, and I understand if that shifts how we relate. I'm still wishing you well."
- "This isn't anger. It's clarity. And I'm allowed to choose peace over confusion."

▌Digital Boundaries Checklist

Make sure your online spaces align with your emotional health:

- Unfollow accounts that trigger comparison, anxiety, or low self-worth
- Mute or remove digital access from toxic people—even if you know them in real life
- Set app limits or tech-free time to reconnect with yourself
- Don't feel guilty for not responding instantly. You're not a machine—you're a human.

◆ Recommended Books for Further Growth

If *Trade UP* resonated with you, we highly recommend:

- Attached by Amir Levine & Rachel Heller — Understand your attachment style and how it impacts relationships
- Set Boundaries, Find Peace by Nedra Glover Tawwab — Practical boundary-setting techniques
- All About Love by bell hooks — A revolutionary exploration of what real love is
- The Mountain Is You by Brianna Wiest — Deep work on self-sabotage, healing, and personal power
- The Four Agreements by Don Miguel Ruiz — Foundational principles for inner peace and strong relationships

✘ Next Steps

If you're serious about applying what you've learned:

1. Revisit the reflection prompts at the end of each chapter.
2. Pick one boundary this week and practice enforcing it.
3. Audit your top 5 closest relationships using the Relationship Alignment Audit.
4. Share this book with someone who needs it—and start a real conversation.
5. Don't just read. Act. Heal. Choose better. Stay up.

Final Reflections

"You don't rise by chance. You rise by choice."

By now, you've explored how to evaluate your relationships, protect your peace, raise your standards, heal your heart, and attract connections that reflect the person you're becoming.

But this journey doesn't end with the last page.

This is where it *really* begins.

Because what you've just read is not just a book—it's a mirror.
A mirror to see your patterns.
A mirror to see your worth.
A mirror to see your future if you stop settling and start choosing *with clarity.*

You Are the Standard Now

You no longer need to beg for love.
You no longer need to over-explain your boundaries.
You no longer need to fit into relationships that don't fit your future.

Let this truth sink in:

You are not hard to love. You were just loving in the wrong direction.

From this moment on, you set the tone.
You decide the access.
You choose what stays, what grows, and what gets released.

You've Already Won

If you made it through this book with honesty, self-reflection, and even a little discomfort...
You've already started the process of *trading up.*

You've already:

- Released old cycles
- Set new standards
- Seen yourself more clearly
- Declared that "peace is more valuable than history"

Don't underestimate that. This is the work most people run from. And you walked straight through it.

Your Future Is Full of Better

Better friendships.
Better love.
Better boundaries.
Better decisions.
Better peace.

But only if you stay honest. Stay grounded. Stay aligned.

You don't owe anyone access to the version of you that no longer exists.

From now on...

- Choose peace over pressure.
- Choose alignment over attention.
- Choose healing over habit.
- Choose clarity over chaos.
- Choose yourself without apology.

Because the love you're looking for—the real thing—*starts with you.*

Thank you for reading, reflecting, and rising with us. We believe in your growth. We believe in your ability to choose better. And we believe that the next chapter of your life will be built on truth, peace, and power.

Now go write it. — Dominic Weeks & Shaun Phillips

Made in the USA
Middletown, DE
17 January 2026

26897104R00031